CW01640421

Copyright © 2022 Meonatrip
All Rights Reserved. No part of this publication may be reproduced, stored in a retrieval system, or transmitted, in any form or in any means – by electronic, mechanical, photocopying, recording or otherwise – without prior written permission. Disclaimer: Although the author and Meonatrip have taken all reasonable care in preparing this book, we make no warranty about the accuracy or completeness of its content and, to the maximum extent permitted, disclaim all liability arising from its use.

LEARN ABOUT CANADA

For Kids

Learn About Canada Contents

Learn About Canada Contents

Where is Canada?

Canada is in North America and is bordered by only one other country; the United States. Canada has three coasts: the Pacific to the west, the Atlantic to the east, and the Arctic to the north.

Fun Fact: It is believed that the name Canada originated from the Huron-Iroquois word "kanata", which means "village" or "settlement".

Provinces and Territories

Canada has ten provinces and three territories. The difference between a province and a territory is how they are governed.

Provinces have certain constitutional powers, while the powers in each territory are given to them under the authority of the Parliament of Canada. This means each provincial government has more specific rights and powers than the territories.

Fun Fact: There are six time zones in Canada.

The Language

Canada has two official languages: English and French. The province with the most Francophones (people who speak French) is Québec, with 85.4% of its population. New Brunswick also has a high percentage of Francophones, with 31.8%. However, after that, most Canadians are Anglophones (people who speak English). Even though Canada is bilingual, less than 18% of the entire country can speak both languages fluently.

All official government documents must be made available in both English and French.

Fun Fact: Canada is a multi-cultural country, with people from all over the world immigrating there. By 2021, one in eight Canadians (12.5%) spoke a language other than French or English at home. For this reason, government offices try to make important documents available in many languages to serve the immigrant population.

Québec Language Laws

The Province of Québec has some strict language laws to protect the French language culture. The Province introduced a law that all businesses must offer their services in French. No matter how big or small, companies must have a French business name. They can also have a name in another language, including English, but they must apply for permission.

Advertising must be in French. This includes ads on the sides of buses, billboards, and store windows. There can be English or another language, but the French portion must be at least twice as big.

In Québec, all road signs are in French only.

Money in Canada

Canadian notes (bills) are made from polymer, which feels like paper with a plastic coating. Polymer replaced paper notes in 2011 because it lasts longer, is environmentally friendly (recyclable) and enables more security features.

Fun Fact: Canadians put so many security features into their money that there is a rumour that the maple leaf on the $100 bill is scratch-and-sniff and smells like maple syrup. Spoiler alert: it's not true.

Canada stopped using pennies in 2013. In 1987, they stopped using one-dollar bills and created a gold-coloured coin affectionately called "the loonie" because there is a picture of a loon (Ontario's official bird) on it. What do you think they called it when they replaced the two-dollar bill with a coin? Why a TWO-NIE (or TOONIE), of course!

The Canadian Flag

Introduced in 1965, the Candian flag features a maple leaf in the centre. The maple leaf has been a symbol of Canadian identity since the 19th century. Indigenous peoples valued it for the sweet syrup the maple tree produced and the goods they made from the wood.

The flag used to include the union jack and Canada's coat of arms (see below). But Canada wanted to have a flag that was unique and independent from their British roots.

Fun Fact: In 1956, the Canadian flag caused quite a misunderstanding in Egypt. They were being invaded by Israel, France and the United Kingdom, so Canadian troops came to Egypt as peacekeepers. But because the union jack was on their flag, it looked like Canada was siding with the United Kingdom. This further reinforced the idea that Canada really should have a unique flag of their own.

The Weather in Canada

Fun Fact: About 90% of Canadians live within 150 km (93 miles) of the United States border.

Canada is the second largest country in the world, but most of the land is uninhabited. In the north, the weather is too cold, and the ground isn't suitable for farming.

The weather in Canada also differs from the west coast, where it is warmer and rainier, to the east coast, where it is colder and dryer. Canada experiences cold, snowy winters and warm (sometimes hot) sunny summers. They enjoy all four seasons with budding trees and rainy days in the spring and beautiful fall colours in autumn.

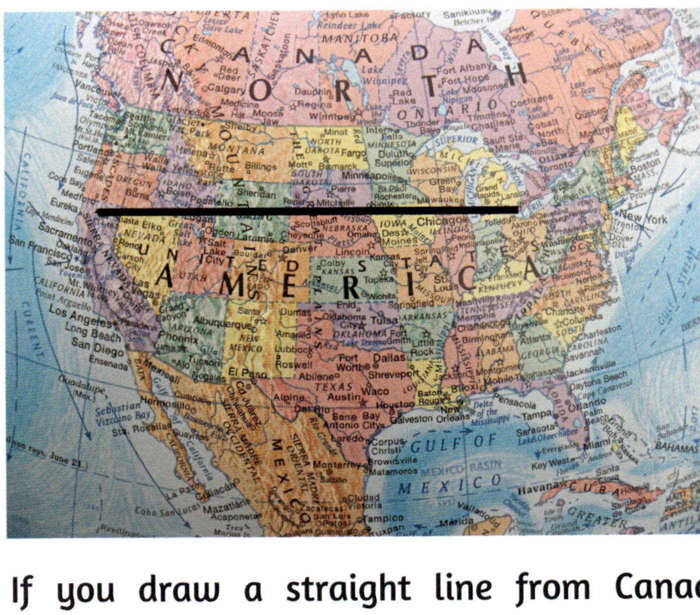

Fun Fact: If you draw a straight line from Canada's most southern city, Windsor, Ontario, you will end up in Northern California in the U.S. Look at the picture above, and you'll see that a good portion of the lower 48 States is further north than heavily populated cities of Ontario and Quebec.

Natural Disasters in Canada

Natural disasters like earthquakes and hurricanes, for example, are rare in Canada. Of the 171 countries ranked, Canada is #27 to be the safest from a natural disaster. In 2016, there was a 3.01% chance of a disaster. This is comparable to the United States, with a 3.76% chance, and the United Kingdom, with a 3.54%. Mexico had a 5.97% chance, and the most vulnerable country was Vanuatu, with 36.28%.

The most common natural disaster in Canada is flooding, most often caused by heavy rainfall. It's not so much that they get a lot of rain, but when the ground is frozen or partly frozen in the colder months, it can't absorb the rain as fast. Flooding can also be caused in the spring when a particularly warm day might melt the winter snow too fast and can't drain quickly enough.

The Population of Canada

As of 2022, the population of Canada was about 38,537,000 people and represented only 0.48% of the world's population.

23% (almost one in every 4 Canadians) immigrated to Canada from another country*. Canada depends on immigration because more Canadians live longer and have fewer children, so they rely on immigrants to fill available jobs and contribute to the economy.

*Source: Statistics Canada, 2022

Population Density

Population density refers to the number of people living within one square kilometre (km) by dividing a country's total population by total land area.

Let's compare countries:

Country	**Population Density per sq. km.**
United States	37
United Kingdom	279
Bangladesh	1,315
Denmark	147
Australia	3
Taiwan	660
Germany	239
Italy	200
France	118
Spain	95
Mexico	66
Singapore	8,323
Iceland	4
Canada	4

Is your country listed above? Is your country's population more or less dense than Canada's?

But keep in mind that the numbers represent the **entire** country. Although the population density is 4 in all of Canada, when you look at its biggest city, Toronto, the population density per 1 km is 1,051 people!

What Kind of Homes do Canadian People Live in?

More than half of the Canadian population (52.6%) live in a single, detached home. 5% live in a semi-detached house, and 6.5% live in a row house. As for apartments, 5.5% of Canadians live in a duplex apartment, 18.3% live in a low-rise apartment building, 10.7% live in high-rises, and the rest of the population (1.4%) live in movable dwellings (trailers, for example). These figures come from the 2021 census.

So how many Canadians live in an igloo? None. Igloos are used by northern Canadian Inuits and American and Russian Eskimos as temporary shelters when hunting or travelling. We only included the picture on the left page to trick you :)

Where Does Everyone Live?

It was mentioned earlier that 90% of Canadians live within 150 km of the United States border. But it's a big border, so let's break it down further.

Toronto is Canada's largest city, and the Greater Toronto Area (GTA) has a population of about 6,313,000. This makes Toronto the 7th largest city in all of North America. It's a little bit bigger than Miami, Florida.

Montreal is North America's 19th largest city, with a population of just over four million people, and it's just a little bigger than Rome, Italy. Canada's third largest city is Vancouver, North America's 31st largest city, a little bigger than Paris, France.

Fun Fact: The Canada/U.S border is the longest international border in the world.

Calgary, Alberta

St. Anthony, Newfoundland

Ottawa, Ontario

Lunenburg, Nova Scotia

Canadian Schools

The Government of Canada (federal government) oversees education. However, each Province can make rules around school hours and holidays, for example.

Canada has a public and a private system for all three levels of education (elementary or primary school, high school and college/university). Public education for elementary and high school is entirely free. Homeschooling is legal across Canada, with each Province making the rules. Some provinces help to fund homeschooling.

Fun Fact: Canada is the most educated country in the world. 90% of Canadians have completed at least high school (including an equivalent for homeschoolers), and more than 56% have completed a post-secondary education with a college diploma or university degree.

Source: Organization for Economic Cooperation and Development (OECD)- residents ages 25-64 who have completed some form of post-secondary education.

Elementary School

Also called primary school, it starts in kindergarten or grade one and goes to grade 8. The school year begins in September and ends in June.

Public schools in Canada do not require students to wear a uniform. However, many private and religious schools do.

High School

High school starts in grade 9 and goes to Grade 12 (Ontario has an extra year that is optional for University preparation). Unlike Americans, Canadians do not refer to freshmen (grade 9), sophomores (grade 10), juniors (grade 11) or seniors (grade 12).

Post-Secondary School

In Canada, there is a difference between university and college. You would earn a degree from a university, but from college, you could get a combination of degrees, diplomas, post-graduate diplomas and certificates. College is usually a 2-3 year program, while university typically takes 4-5 years to complete. Some college credits can be transferred to a university if the student changes their mind and decides to pursue a university degree instead of a college diploma.

In Québec, the province funds a 2-year program for students aged 16 - 18. It is intended to prepare the student for university. This is a separate school called a CEGEP (pronounced see-jep).

Public Transit in Canada

Public transit is the responsibility of each city or municipality, so it differs from place to place and depends on the town's size. Let's look at Canada's largest city, Toronto.

Toronto uses buses, subways and streetcars to get around. The red streetcars are an iconic part of the city.

Special Transit

Canada's laws ensure that people with disabilities have access to transit. Public transportation always includes features like spaces for wheelchairs and ramps. For people with disabilities in Toronto, Wheel trans will come to their door on an appointment, so they don't have to go to a bus stop.

School Buses in Canada are yellow and are free for students who live a certain distance from their school.

The Landscapes of Canada

Canada has some of the most beautiful landscapes in the world.
Fun Fact: The Great Lakes in Ontario is the world's largest body of freshwater by area.

Forests

Countryside

Lakes

Mountains

Prairies

Beaches

The Most Photographed Places in Canada

Stanley Park, Vancouver

Moraine Lake Alberta

Niagara Falls, Ontario

Some Wild Animals That Live in Canada

Polar Bear

Beaver
(more on page 41)

Moose

21

Bison

Some Wild Birds That Live in Canada

Canada Goose

Puffin

Blue Jay & Grey Jay

Loon

The Biggest Industries in Canada

Manufacturing & Technology

Agriculture

Lumber

Energy

Oil and Gas

Maple Syrup

Fun Fact: Although it isn't on the list of Canada's biggest industries, it's interesting to know that 75% of all the maple syrup in the world comes from Canada. The rest comes from the northern United States.

Most of the syrup comes from Québec. They tap the maple trees and let the sap drip into buckets. After filtering the sap, it is cooked to become syrup. This is only done in late winter/early spring, and they make a massive deal of the whole thing with Sugaring Off parties.

Ottawa, the Capital of Canada

Ottawa is located in Ontario, near the Quebec border.

The parliament buildings (pictured above) were built between 1859 and 1866. Then in 1867, Canada became a country.

Toronto, the Capital of Ontario

Toronto sits on the north shore of Lake Ontario. It is considered the banking and economic centre of Canada and is also the most visited city in the country. It's located 450 km (280 miles) south of Ottawa and only 128 km (80 miles) north of Niagara Falls.

An easy city to recognise in photos, the iconic CN Tower is always a standout.

For more on the CN Tower, go to page 62.

The Maritimes

New Brunswick, Nova Scotia, and Prince Edward Island make up the Maritime Provinces. Maritime refers to the sea, and the Maritimes are along the Atlantic coast where Canada's fishing industry lives.

The culture is distinctive - many residents there have roots in Ireland, Scotland and the United Kingdom, mixed in with some Acadian French, which shows in their unique accents. Maritimers are known for their incredible hospitality and friendliness. If you are lucky enough to visit the Maritimes, check out the icebergs, the whales, and the lighthouses.

The Maritimes are also known for the harsh weather, especially hurricanes. Most recently, in September 2022, the Maritimes were hit by Hurricane Fiona. The Insurance Bureau of Canada reported that this was the most costly storm in Atlantic Canada's history, with over $660 million in damages. The violent winds and rainfall knocked out power to more than half a million homes in the Maritimes.

Hurricane Earl at Peggy's Cove, Nova Scotia 2016

The Prairie Provinces

Manitoba, Saskatchewan and Alberta make up the Prairie Provinces. This is where much of Canada's agriculture is, with livestock (primarily cattle and sheep) and crops (mostly oats, canola, wheat and barley). The prairies are also rich in Alberta's oil production, making Canada one of the top petroleum exporters in the world.

The Prairies have a distinct cowboy culture, especially in southern Calgary. Country Western music is familiar there, and rodeos are a popular event. In particular, the famous Calgary Stampede takes place every July for ten days. The Stampede is over 100 years old and sees more than a million visitors every summer. Although the rodeo is the show's star, people also attend the midway, agricultural fairgrounds, concerts, chuckwagon races and First Nations exhibitions. The Calgary Stampede is a uniquely Canadian experience.

The Northern Territories

Yukon, Northwest Territories and Nunavut make up Canada's territories. The land mass makes up 39.1% of Canada, but the population is 0.3%*. Conditions in these areas are far too harsh compared to the lower provinces, but some of those who live there wouldn't want to be elsewhere.

Most people are surprised to find out there's a city in the territories - it's called Yellowknife, with a population of more than 20,000 people. What makes Yellowknife famous is that it is considered by some to be the best place in the world to view the Aurora Borealis, also known as The Northern Lights. More about that is on page 33.

The average temperature in Yellowknife ranges from -29C (-21F) in the winter to 22C (71F)* in the summer. The Northwest territories have several beaches where the locals do ordinary things like swim, camp and play volleyball.

Yellowknife, Northwest Territories in the summer

*Source: Statistics Canada , February 2022

Newfoundland and Labrador

Although it sounds like two places, Newfoundland and Labrador is the name of one province. The island portion is Newfoundland, and the mainland portion is Labrador. In 2001, the name was made official, but most people just call it Newfoundland since almost 95% of the province's population lives on the island.

Fun Fact: The proper way to pronounce Newfoundland Is:

Noo-fn-Land

Some people accentuate the "new" part, others emphasize "land", and either is OK, so long as you don't pay much attention to the "found" part. That part is always pronounced "fn".

If you're lucky enough to visit Newfoundland, you should attend a Screeched-In Ceremony. Newfoundlanders are such a friendly bunch; they have a ceremony for all first-time visitors so they can become "Honorary Newfoundlanders". The ritual involves eating a piece of bologna, kissing a dead codfish on the lips, and drinking a shot of screech (a type of rum). But don't worry, they have a kid version with rum cake instead of rum. Once you do these things, you will be asked, "Is ye a screecher?" and you must answer:

> "Deed I is, me old b'y, and long may your big
> jib draw!"

Translated, this means, "yes, I am, my old friend, and may there always be wind in your sails".

Fun Fact: Newfoundland is the foggiest place in the world.

British Columbia

British Columbia is Canada's westernmost province and is well-known for its beautiful nature and outdoor adventures like hiking, canoeing, camping and skiing. It's like Canada's playground. British Columbia is probably Canada's most beautiful province. There are six national parks and the Rocky Mountains (the Canadian Rockies in northern British Columbia).

Stanley Park, Vancouver, is the most visited attraction in British Columbia and is famous for its First Nations Totem Poles. The original poles were carved as early as 1880. Sadly, 100 years later, they started to rot and fade, so the ones there now are replicas. Totem poles were first created by the First Nations peoples of the area and are symbols that represent ancestry, history, people or events. Each character on a totem pole has a special meaning.

Indigenous Peoples - Truth & Reconciliation

Indigenous or Aboriginal peoples include First Nations, Inuit and Métis. Each group have a unique history, culture, language and spiritual beliefs. According to the 2021 census, 1.8 million Canadians identify as Indigenous.

First Nations: Canada has more than 630 First Nation communities, and they represent more than 50 Nations and languages.

Inuit: The Inuit language is called Inuktitut, and Inuit means "the people". Inuit peoples live in the Arctic.

Métis: Mainly aboriginal peoples from the Prairie provinces, Métis are also in British Columbia and Ontario.

Canada has had a shameful past in trying to force a different culture onto the indigenous population. The government did this by taking indigenous children from their homes and families and making them live in residential schools run by the catholic church. The schools forced the children to unlearn their culture and language. Only recently has the government recognised its past crimes against the indigenous and has begun a process of "truth and reconciliation". The Truth is to educate all Canadians about the past and Reconciliation to try and heal. September 30th was declared in 2021 as a national holiday known as Truth and Reconciliation Day, or Orange Shirt Day, so Canadians can reflect and learn. The orange shirt symbolises one particular story about a child who wore an orange shirt on her first day at a residential school. The shirt was a gift from her grandmother. She was forced to get rid of it and wear a uniform instead.

Aurora Borealis or The Northern Lights

The Aurora Borealis is caused by particles from the sun interacting with the earth's magnetic field. It can only be seen in the earth's northern hemisphere, although the southern hemisphere has the aurora australis or southern lights.

The Northern Lights are visible year-round, but you have a better chance of seeing them in the winter. The further north you go, the better. They don't occur every night, so many people book a Northern Lights holiday where they stay for 4-5 days to increase their chances.

The Aurora Borealis can be seen from other countries besides Canada, like Norway, Lapland, Iceland and Greenland.

Chinooks

Also known as "snow-eaters", chinooks are a winter weather phenomenon in southern Alberta. It can turn a cold winter day into a hot one in just a matter of hours. It happens when strong winds blow cold air from the Pacific coast up the western slope of the Rocky Mountains, where the air warms, then blows down the eastern slope into Calgary, bringing the warm air with it.

You can literally see a chinook by the cloud it forms. Called the Chinook Arch.

The most extreme example of a chinook happened in 1962 when the temperature at Pincher Creek, Alberta, went from -19c (-2f) to 22c (71.6f) in just one hour!

Canadian Police

One of the stereotypes of Canada is the Royal Canadian Mounted Police, or RCMP. The police are often nicknamed "mounties".

The RCMP is Canada's national police force, and they ride on horses. Sometimes. But the RCMP do not hang around on a horse in every city and town in red uniforms, chasing crooks and handing out speeding tickets.

Almost all cities and towns in Canada have a municipal police service that wears navy blue uniforms and mostly rides in cars (although some ride bikes, motorcycles, boats and horses).

The RCMP provides national security and intelligence gathering, similar to the FBI in the United States, Europol in Europe, or M15 in Great Britain.

The RCMP Musical Ride performs across Canada on special occasions. There are up to 32 officers who perform with their horses as a symbol of Canadian tradition, honour and pride.

Canada's Spy Agency

Like in other countries, Canada has its spy agency (better known as an intelligence agency). Their role is to protect Canada from outside security threats. In Canada, this agency is called CSIS (see-sis). The letters stand for Canadian Security Intelligence Service. This would be equivalent to the CIA in the United States, the EU INTCEN in Europe, or the M16 in the United Kingdom.

Fun Fact: You'll notice on page 35 a reference to the police *service*. In Canada, they never call it a police *force*. That's an important distinction.

Canada's Ties to the British Monarchy

Canada used to be a colony of the British Empire but became self-governing in 1867, although it kept ties with Britain by remaining The Dominion of Canada. Dominion status means that Canada is a self-governing nation of the British Empire. Other Dominion countries include South Africa, Australia and New Zealand.

In 1931, Canada became a member of the British Commonwealth. The British Commonwealth is an association of 56 countries. Most members have historical ties to Britain, but not all. The member countries owe an allegiance to the King or Queen of England (the Monarch) but are not ruled by them. Members of the Commonwealth are simply an alliance of countries that recognise the Crown (the British monarchy).

At the recommendation of Canada's Prime Minister, the Crown appoints a Governor General to Canadian Parliament. The Governor General's job is to represent the Crown's interests by reading the Throne's Speech, giving Royal Assent (approval from the Crown), and bringing parliamentary bills into law. The Governor General appoints a Lieutenant Governor for each province. A Lieutenant Governor is the highest-ranking officer of the province they represent.

Fun Fact: Canada pays over 55 million dollars to the Crown every year. It sounds like a lot, but when you break it down, it's only about $1.25 per Canadian per year. This money goes to the Governor General to pay for their offices and to carry out their duties. It also goes toward visits to Canada from the Royal Family. But none of the money goes directly to the Royal Palace.

Canada's Only Neighbour

Canada has a fantastic relationship with its only neighbour, the United States. The Canada Border Services Agency (CBSA) and the U.S. Customs and Border Protection (CBP) ensure these two neighbours can travel back and forth without much of a problem. In fact, many Canadians work in the U.S., and many Americans work in Canada.

To make travel even more accessible, the two neighbours created the Nexus program, also known as the Trusted Traveler program. Citizens of either country can apply to the CBSA and the CBP to have a Nexus card. As long as you have a valid passport, no criminal record, and pass a personal interview with both agencies, you can get a card. This card lets you travel across the border even easier.

However, the relationship between the two countries has only sometimes been so friendly. The United States invaded Canada twice; in 1775 during the American Revolution and the Battle of Québec and again in 1812 during the War of 1812.

During the American Revolution, the United States was fighting Great Britain. The U.S. invaded Québec and tried to persuade the citizens to join them against Great Britain, but they weren't successful.

In 1812 the U.S. invaded Canada again, and the battles took place mainly in Niagara. Again, this was more directed at Great Britain than Canada. Once again, the Americans lost because the Royal Navy, the British Army, Canadian militia and the First Peoples warriors greatly outnumbered them.

Immigration

Immigration is when people from other countries move in. Canada has an immigration policy that makes rules around who is allowed to move there and who isn't.

Canada depends on its immigrants to keep the population up and to have people contribute to the economy. Canada works hard to ensure that immigrants are treated fairly and are respected within their communities. They take pride in being a welcoming country and in the fact that Canada is one of the most diverse countries in the world.

According to the 2021 census, 23% of Canadians were immigrants. Most of these people are from India, the Philippines, and China.

So we know why Canada wants immigrants, but why do people want to move there? Besides being a great country to live in, the biggest reasons are:

- to be with family
- for work
- to escape war or bad conditions

Even though Canada loves immigrants, there are some rules to living there. For example, you cannot move to Canada if you have no way to support yourself, have bad health, or have a criminal record.

Mosaic vs Melting Pot

The mosaic art piece in this picture perfectly describes the Canadian attitude toward immigrants. Each piece represents an ethnic group that maintains its identity and culture but, placed all together, contributes to making a beautiful picture and society.

On the other hand, some countries reject the mosaic ideal and prefer to see their immigration policy as more of a "melting pot". This means they want all people to contribute to society, not as individuals but as a part of society as a whole.

There are arguments about whether a mosaic or a melting pot is best. Canada is so convinced that a mosaic is an ideal that there are laws that protect cultural identity. Canadians are encouraged to celebrate significant events across the country, celebrating different, unique cultures.

Famous Canadian Inventions

basketball

insulin

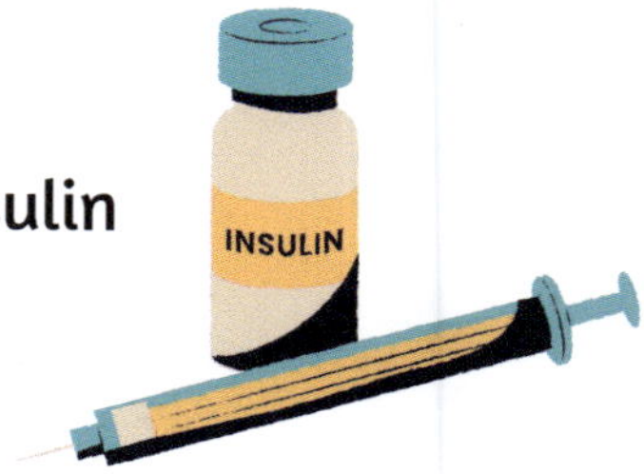

paint roller

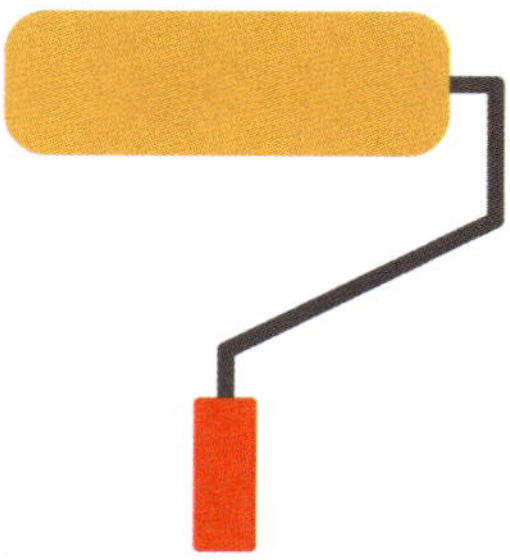

electric wheelchair

garbage bags

peanut butter

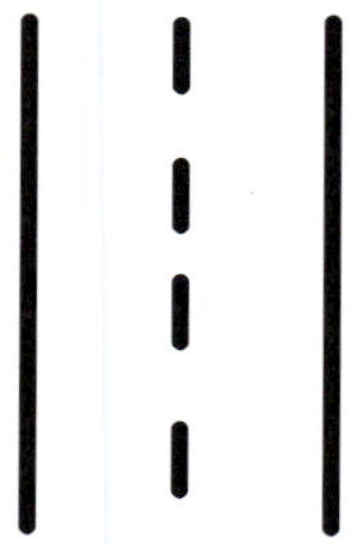

road lines

IMAX theatre

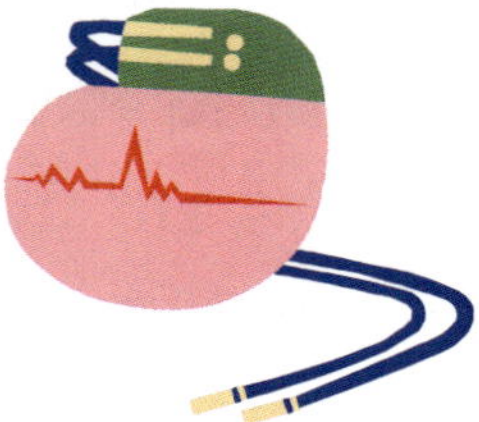

pacemaker

fibreglass goalie mask

The Canadarm

In the early 1970s, the National Aeronautics and Space Administration (NASA) in the United States had a problem. They were developing the Space Shuttle but needed a way of unloading its contents while in space.

The Canadian Space Agency came to the rescue with the invention of a robotic arm. Very proud of this fantastic invention, they named it the "Canadarm" and painted "Canada" on it.

The robot arm is made of titanium, stainless steel and graphite epoxy. The original Canadarm is now retired; you can see it at the Canada Aviation and Space Museum in Ottawa, Ontario.

The Beaver - Canada's National Animal

Most countries have a national animal: The U.S. has the bald eagle, England has the lion, India has the tiger, Russia has the bear, and, well, Canada has the beaver. So while other countries choose strong, majestic animals, why would Canada select a buck-toothed rodent?

Canada would not be the country it is today without the beaver. It began with the fur trade in the 16th century. Beaver pelts were an essential part of the country's economy for almost 300 years. Beaver pelts were used to make hats, winter coats and blankets. Also, the beaver lives in every province in Canada, representing the entire country.

Fun Fact: a beaver's front teeth are bucked to chew logs underwater without getting water in their mouth. Their teeth continue to grow for their entire lives, but they chew on wood to keep them a controllable length.

The Grey Jay - Canada's National Bird

After much debate, the Grey Jay, also known as the Whiskey Jack, was named Canada's national bird in 2017 by Canadian Geographic. For two years, Canadian Geographic consulted with Canadian citizens, ornithologists, conservationists, cultural experts, and Canada's Indigenous Peoples before declaring the national bird.

Why the Grey Jay?

- it lives in all 13 provinces and territories
- it's not already an official provincial bird
- it remains in Canada all year round
- except for a small area in the United States, the Grey Jay only lives in Canada and nowhere else in the world
- Canadians know their forests and climate are healthy as long as the Grey Jay is around.

Fun Fact: The Cree First Nations tell a story about a native spirit and shape-shifter called Wisakedjak (Whiskey jack) who will shape-shift into a bird (a grey jay) when he needs to be a teacher or messenger of the forest. To First Nations, seeing a Grey Jay in the morning is good luck. and when a Grey Jay chatters, it's a warning of predators nearby.

Fun Facts About Lakes

- Canada is home to four of the ten largest freshwater lakes in the world. Lake Erie (#10), Great Slave Lake (#9), Great Bear Lake (#7), and Lake Superior (#1).
  *Size is based on the surface area, not volume.

- Wasaga Beach, Ontario, is the longest freshwater beach in the world.

- Manitoulin Island in Ontario is the largest freshwater island in the world.

- 20% of the world's freshwater supply is in Canada.

- Hudson Bay has the lowest gravity in the world.

- The five Great Lakes share borders with the United States. Except for Lake Michigan, which is 100% in the U.S.

- Bessie is a mythical sea monster that lives in Lake Erie—also known as the Lake Erie Monster. People claim they've seen Bessie for decades, but there's no proof.

Why is Lake Louise so Pretty?

Lake Louise in Alberta is known for its beautiful colour. Depending on the time of day and the weather, the colour will be either emerald green or turquoise blue, but both are equally beautiful.

The meltwater from the glacier that feeds the lake (Victoria Glacier) contains rock flour, a fine ground-up powder created from erosion. This rock flour travels with the meltwater and into the ice-cold lake. When the sun reflects the rock flour, it colours this beautiful green/blue water.

Fun Fact: Lake Louise used to be called "Emerald Lake", but in 1884, the name was changed to honour Queen Victoria's daughter, Princess Louise Caroline Alberta. And yes, the province was also named after the Princess.

Unique Canadian Holidays

Canada has some unique holidays besides the regular Christmas, New Year, and other holidays shared with the world. So if you ever travel to Canada, be aware of the following special celebrations and observances:

Monday before May 25 - Victoria Day. Also affectionately known as "May two-four". Officially a statutory holiday (which means children get the day off school and all employers MUST either give the day off work or pay overtime) to celebrate the birth of Queen Victoria. But in reality, Canadians use the holiday to celebrate the upcoming summer season. It's the weekend to "open the cottage" (see page 46), plant the garden, go camping, watch fireworks, and have parties and BBQs with friends and family.

July 1 - Canada Day. This is also a statutory holiday. Canada Day celebrates Canada's Confederation in 1967 and its establishment of dominion status. This is why Canada Day is also sometimes called Dominion Day. Canada Day is typically marked with fireworks, BBQs and parties. If the day falls in the middle of the week, it is often moved to a Monday or Friday so Canadians can make a long weekend of it.

First Monday in September - Labour Day. This public holiday is also statutory and celebrates workers. It's a long weekend celebrating with parades to honour the working class. Labour Day weekend is also famous in Canada for "closing the cottage".

September 30 - Truth & Reconciliation Day - (see page 32).

Cottage Culture

Most Canadians love nature, but some, especially those who live in southern Ontario, don't get enough of it. This is what brought on the cottage culture. If they can afford it, southern Ontarians will buy a cottage "up north" to escape the city and enjoy nature in the summer months. If they can't buy a cottage, there is plenty to rent, which are booked months in advance.

Towns and parks near Georgian Bay and further north to Muskoka are part of "cottage country". Once at the cottage, families and friends enjoy swimming, fishing, hiking, and sitting around a campfire.

Cottage culture is so prevalent in southern Ontario that if anyone who lives there doesn't own a cottage, they likely have a friend or family member who does. They wait for their invitation to "meet up at the cottage".

Winter in Canada

It can get freezing and very snowy in Canada during the winter. But as we learned on page 7, most Canadians live next to the U.S. border, and much of the northern United States is further north than the most populated part of Canada (southern Ontario).

Because Canada is so big, giving a reliable range of typical temperatures or snowfall is impossible. But it is fair to say that most Canadians make the best of winter and enjoy many outdoor activities like skiing, skating, making snow forts, and tobogganing.

Summer in Canada

Canadian summers are enjoyable. Although temperatures often get into the 30s celsius (high 80s Fahrenheit), the mid-20s (70s) are more typical.

Canadians spend their summers camping, cottaging, swimming (so many lakes to choose from!), hiking, BBQing, and just enjoying the season.

Can You Speak Canadian?

Not the language, but more about unique Canadian words. Here are a few Canadianisms you might want to know:

1. **Eh**. Pronounced like the letter A. Although Canadians say it a lot, it isn't just thrown in thoughtlessly. "eh" actually has a definition. It means, "don't you agree?". For example, "this is a fun book about Canada, eh?". When a Canadian says "eh", they expect you to nod, say "yes", or otherwise confirm you agree.

2. **Loonie and Toonie**. A loonie is a one-dollar Canadian coin. It got its name because there is a picture of a loon engraved in it. A toonie is a two-dollar Canadian coin.

3. **Toque**. Pronounced too-k. This is what Canadians call a warm winter cap or beanie.

4. **Washroom**. Americans call it a bathroom, the British call it a lavatory or loo, and other countries can refer to it as a water closet or toilet. In Canada, most people refer to it as a washroom.

5. **Double-Double**. A Canadian says this when ordering a coffee with two cream and two sugar.

6. **Hydro**. Hydro means electricity generated from moving water. Canada, along with Brazil, New Zealand, Norway, and several other countries, gets most of their electricity from hydroelectric power. So in Canada, "hydro" refers to electricity generated from a hydro plant that turns moving water into electricity.

It's pretty cold out there eh?
Yes! That's why I'm wearing my toque
Can I use your washroom please?
Sure, just remember to turn off the lights when you leave, my hydro bill was really high this month.
I found a loonie and a toonie in my desk, can I buy you a coffee?
sure! double double please

Canadian Food - Poutine

Of course, Canadians eat regular food like anywhere else in the world, including meat, fish, fruit, vegetables and dairy. But certain foods are famously Canadian, and dishes you have to try if you visit there.

Number one on the list is poutine (pronounced poo-teen). This is a simple French-Canadian dish made of three ingredients: french fries (chips in the U.K.), cheese curds (cheddar that hasn't aged), and gravy. When you pour hot gravy over the cheese curds, they become chewy, gooey, and delicious.

Fun Fact: The word "poutine" is Québec slang that means "a mess".

Montréal-Style Smoked Meat Sandwiches

A ridiculously tall stack of smoked brisket (like corned beef or pastrami, only fattier) on rye bread spread with mustard and a side of dill pickle will give you a traditional Montréal-style smoked meat sandwich.

Montréal is also famous for their bagels. These bagels are special because they are made by hand and poached in honey water, then baked in a wood-fired oven.

Canadian Food - Tourtiére

Tourtiére (pronounced toor-tyair) is a savoury meat pie, often served as part of a Christmas Eve dinner. The meat is a ground mixture of pork, beef and veal, and the spices include cinnamon, clove and allspice. Every Québec grandmother has a special recipe for tortiére that makes it even more special.

Bannock is a flatbread with its roots in Scotland, but it was adopted by Canadian Indigenous peoples who have made it a staple in Canada.

Canadians Have a Sweet Tooth as Well

Butter tarts have a deep history in Canadian food culture. These delicious little pastries are filled with a mixture of sugar, egg, butter and syrup. Variations include adding pecans or raisins.

Nanaimo (pronounced nan-nime-o) bars are named after the town they were invented in; Nanaimo, British Columbia. These are no-bake bars with a coconutty bottom layer, a yellow custard centre, and a chocolate top layer.

Interesting Tourist Spots for Kids

Dinosaur Provincial Park in Alberta. This park was named after the dinosaur fossil fields, some of the world's largest. Writing-on-Stone / Áísínai'pi is a provincial park also in Alberta. Áísínai'pi means "where the writings are".

The Canadian National Exhibition (CNE)

The CNE marks the end of summer each year in Toronto. It runs for around two weeks, from the end of August to the first weekend of September. Midways, air shows, buskers, agricultural exhibits, and crazy food concoctions mark the CNE. Every year the vendors try to outdo each other for weird food. 2022 saw the introduction of mustard and ketchup-flavoured ice cream!

Niagara Falls

Besides the amazing falls itself - the most Instagrammed waterfall in the world, with over 3.5 million hashtags - the City of Niagara Falls, Ontario, has many fun things to keep you entertained. You can take a boat ride around the base of the falls, check out scary wax museums and ride a giant Ferris wheel. Nearby is an indoor water park and lodge, a butterfly conservatory, and ziplining.

Québec City Winter Carnival

If you are in Quebec in February, you can join in the fun at the Québec City Winter Carnival. They have giant snow sculptures, night parades, ice skating, and a fun carnival atmosphere. You can even get a smoked meat sandwich with a side of poutine!

Whale Watching in Nova Scotia

There are 12 species of whales you could see from Nova Scotia. The best time to go is in summer or fall.

Children's Museum , Gatineau, Quebec

With over 15,000 items to see, this is the largest children's museum in the country. You can go on a virtual trip around the world with their "Great Adventure museum passport".

The Calgary Stampede

See page 28.

Visit the CN Tower

The CN Tower in Toronto, Ontario, is the tallest free-standing structure in the western hemisphere (North and South America). Take the enclosed outdoor elevator up, then enjoy the view! If you're brave enough, you can walk on the glass floor. Then have lunch in the rotating restaurant at the top.

The CN Tower is 553 meters tall (1,815 feet). Compare that to the Eiffel Tower in France, which is only 330 meters (1,082 feet). See more pictures on page 26.

The Most Popular Sports in Canada

1. Ice Hockey
2. Soccer
3. Canadian Football
4. Baseball
5. Lacrosse
6. Golf
7. Curling
8. Basketball
9. Skiing
10. Cricket

Canada's National Sport

In 1859, Canada declared its national sport to be lacrosse. However, as the years went by, every Canadian knew the country was equally famous for ice hockey. So in 1994, the government of Canada declared that lacrosse was their national summer sport, and ice hockey was their national winter sport.

Sports - Fun Facts

- Lacross has Indigenous roots - played 500 years ago by different First Nations teams.

- The oldest golf club in all of North America is the Royal Montreal Golf Club, founded in 1873.

- Although Basketball is far more popular in the United States, it was invented by Canadian James Naismith in 1891. Mr Naismith was a teacher and needed to find a way for his students to exercise indoors during the winter months. The first basketball game was played using a peach basket at each end of the court and a soccer ball.

- A Canadian football field is bigger than an American football field. These two countries also play by different rules, which is why you often hear a distinction between the terms "American football" and "Canadian football".

- In Europe, football refers to soccer. They don't play American or Canadian "football" there. But Canadians call soccer "soccer". Are you confused yet?

- Although Austria, China, Denmark, Japan, Spain, Russia and the United States have curling teams, 90% of the world's curlers live in Canada.

- Canada set the record for the most gold medals in the winter Olympics. This happened in 2010 when Canada won 14 golds.

Mohawk Nations Lacrosse Champions - 1869

Royal Montreal Golf Club - 1896

Canadians Can Be a Superstitious Bunch

At the 2002 Olympics in Salt Lake City, Utah, a Canadian company was hired to lay down the ice at the hockey rink. They secretly placed a loonie under centre ice to bring good luck to the Canadian teams. By the way, the men's and the women's Canadian hockey teams won gold that year.

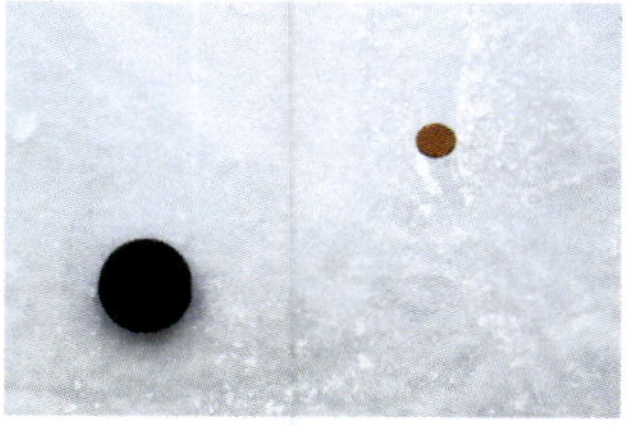

Don't wear grey mittens on a ship. Doing so will invite death.

Before moving into a new home - smudge it to invite positive energy.

In Alberta, don't pick blackberries after Oct 11; those belong to the devil.

In Manitoba, you'll disappear if you run around St. Andrews Church three times at midnight.

10 Funniest Laws in Canada

Every country has some strange laws still on the books. Canada is no exception. Although they are no longer enforced, they remain as laws today. Here are ten of the funniest:

1. It's illegal to scare the queen.

2. You cannot create, possess or sell crime comics.

3. You cannot challenge or accept a challenge to a duel.

4. You cannot use a dog sled on a sidewalk.

5. In Ottawa, Ontario, you cannot eat ice cream outdoors on Bank Street on Sunday (oddly specific!)

6. In Alberta, you are not allowed to paint a wooden ladder.

7. In Toronto, Ontario it is illegal to swear in a public park.

8. In Oshawa, Ontario it is illegal to climb a tree.

9. In Petrolia, Ontario, whistling is illegal.

10. Your snowman must not be more than 76 cm (30 inches) tall.

Pets in Canada

Canadians love their animals. In fact, Canada has one of the highest percentages of pet owners in the world. So what's the favourite? Cats? Dogs? Well, they are close, but cats are a bit more popular than dogs. 38% of Canadian households own a cat, and 35% own a dog. There are also more than a million pet birds in Canada. Hamsters and guinea pigs are also popular.

In Canada, you can have as many pets as you want as long as you take good care of them. Animal rights are taken seriously there.

Bringing Your Pet to Canada

You can bring your dog into Canada as long as they are vaccinated against rabies. You have to have a rabies certificate written in either English or French. The certificate must be issued and signed by a licensed veterinarian and must give the vaccination date plus the vaccine's serial number.

As for your cat, if you come from a country recognised as rabies-free, then all is good, and you can bring him. Otherwise, you'll need to arrange for a rabies vaccine before you arrive and get the same certificate mentioned for a dog. Rabies-free countries include England, Australia, Ireland, and New Zealand. The United States is not on the list, so an American cat must get vaccinated to enter Canada.

After learning so much about Canada, I guess you can understand why it is one of the friendliest countries in the world. Canada loves to welcome visitors, and it's a very safe country for a family to visit. The only problem is that it's so big, you can't see it all in just one visit, so come back again and again!

Acknowldegements:

Pg 4 "Québec Autoroute 50" by Dougtone is licensed under CC BY-SA 2.0.
Pg 6 "File:Hypothetical Current Canadian Red Ensign.svg" by The CSOTK is licensed under CC BY-SA 4.0.
Pg 17 "A Toronto city bus runs through the historic district" by shankar s. is licensed under CC BY 2.0.
Pg 18 Wheel Trans CC0 1.0 Universal (CC0 1.0) Public Domain Dedication
Pg 28 "Barrel Racing at the Calgary Stampede" by Calgary Reviews is licensed under CC BY 2.0.
Pg 34 "File:Chinook Arch - panoramio (1).jpg" by Jack Borno is licensed under CC BY-SA 3.0.
Pg 36 "Toronto Police Service 53 Division Supervisor 3" by GTA Emergency_Photography is licensed under CC BY 2.0.
Pg 44 "Canadarm over Canadian winter" by ESA_events is licensed under CC BY-SA 2.0.
Pg 48 "Lake Louise, Banff National Park" by eleephotography is licensed under CC BY 2.0.
Pg 56 "Montreal Bagels" by eekim is licensed under CC BY 2.0.
Pg 59 "Hoodoos at sunset in Dinosaur Provincial Park/Demoiselles au coucher du soleil, parc provincial Dinosaur, Alberta" by jonebabana is licensed under CC BY 2.0.
Pg 59 "Writing on Stone Provincial Park" by jan_mosimann is licensed under CC BY-ND 2.0.
Pg 60 "Niagara Falls" by VV Nincic is licensed under CC BY 2.0.
Pg 60 "Quebec City Winter Carnival" by Marc-Lautenbacher CC BY-SA 4.0
Pg 61 "A Moment: The Children's Museum" by QUOI Media is licensed under CC BY-SA 2.0.
Pg 66 "Men from the Mohawk Nation at Kahnawake (Caughnawaga) who were the Canadian lacrosse champions in 1869 / Des hommes de la nation mohawk à Kahnawake (Caughnawaga), les champions de la crosse au Canada en 1869" by BiblioArchives / LibraryArchives is licensed under CC BY 2.0.
Pg 66 "Royal Montreal Golf Club 1896" by The Royal Montreal Golf Club is licensed under CC BY-SA 4.0.
Pg 67 "St. Andrew's Church" by Dano is licensed under CC BY 2.0.

About the Author

Collette Valliear is a world-traveller and proud G-Mom to Julien and Beau! She loves to write about travelling and is excited to help inspire others to embrace their inner vagabond. Collette has visited all seven continents and looks forward to taking her grandsons on some epic adventures one day! They love to request books and contribute new ideas often. Collette, a former property manager in Toronto, Canada, turned her retirement into a new chapter of adventure and creativity!

To see more books by Meonatrip, scan the QR code below.

Please leave an honest review on Amazon; it will go a long way to creating more books like this one.

MEONATRIP
2022

Printed in Great Britain
by Amazon

36974824R00048